The Beginner Investor's Guide: Stocks, Cryptocurrencies, Bonds, ETFs and More

Invaluable Stock Market Investing Tips for Beginners

PENNY WOOD

"In the business world, the rearview mirror is always clearer than the windshield."

- Warren Buffett

CONTENTS

CONTENTS

INTRODUCTION

Would you like to invest in stocks, cryptocurrency, or bonds but are not sure where to start? If so, you are not alone. Experienced investors did not know where to invest when they started. Over the years, they not only learned where to invest their money, but also how to select the right stocks, exchange-traded funds, and bonds.

You are now holding a book that was written to answer important questions for beginner investors like you. I will explain in detail what this book covers.

Beginner investors are often unsure of which investment instruments to select for their portfolios. Although every investor's situation is different, there are certain assets that form most people's portfolios. Chapter 1 takes you through various investment instruments including stocks, cryptocurrencies, bonds, exchange-traded funds, and mutual funds. We will use investment instruments and assets interchangeably.

For each of these assets, you will discover what it is, returns realized in the past, and how they can potentially influence future returns. Chapter 1 essentially covers the basic information that you need before you select assets to invest in. You need to know how to open a brokerage account. This is a special account dedicated to holding and trading your investment assets. Like a savings account, you should select a brokerage account that meets your needs and supports your overall investment goals. In Chapter 1, I explain how to determine your selection criteria and what steps to take.

Armed with this information, you may decide to invest in one or more assets. Deciding on your investment goals is the first step (or starting point) to investing. You need to figure out why you want to invest. Your goals may be short-, mid-, or long-term. Chapter 2 explains how to set your investment goals using the *SMART* goal-setting technique. Once you know what you want to achieve, you move on to figure out your risk tolerance. Risk Tolerance refers to the amount of investment-loss uncertainty that you are willing to accept. This is important because the decisions that you'll make going forward will be based on your investment objectives and risk tolerance.

Next, I show you how to allocate the funds in your portfolio. This only applies if you'll be investing in two or more different assets. For a lower risk and *good* return, you need to invest in more than one kind of instrument. Depending on your risk tolerance, you may choose a conservative, aggressive, or any other portfolio in between. The portfolio you choose should be geared to deliver the results that you want. I will explain more about the portfolio types in Chapter 2.

Having decided on a portfolio, your next move is to select assets suitable to drive it to the desired destination. Arguably, the most important assets in most investors' portfolios are stocks. As a result, I show you how to value stocks. This will help you identify overpriced stock. Importantly, you'll be able to select stocks that are underpriced or at a discount. Furthermore, you'll discover a description of the valuation methods you can use. This chapter wouldn't be complete without discussing fundamental and technical analyses. Of these, you'll use fundamental analysis to select which stocks to invest in, while technical analysis will help you to time your entry and exit.

This Chapter explains why you need to diversify your portfolio. You can put your eggs in one basket, but the basket may be stolen, or it may fall and break all the eggs. However, putting your eggs in several baskets improves their changes of producing chicks. Also, I'll take you through a process for selecting each of the investment assets.

Chapter 3 involves managing the portfolio that you create. Why is this important? There are many factors that can affect the performance of the assets in your portfolio. For example, the market may change from a bear to a bullish phase. This, in turn, would impact the performance of some of your assets. As a result, your risk tolerance may be out of sync without your resulting asset allocation. As such, you run the risk of failing to meet your investment goals.

Other changes that could happen include your employment status, marital situation, death in the family, or other life events. These changes could affect your investment objectives and therefore, your risk tolerance. Again, you'll need to adjust your asset allocation to cater to the new situation. The process you use to bring your asset allocation back in line with your original objectives is called rebalancing. There are two ways you can rebalance your portfolio. One involves selling the highest-performing asset and buying more of the lowest-performing securities. This second involves adding more capital to your portfolio. I explain how to apply both rebalancing strategies with detailed examples.

The chapter concludes by looking at how taxes impact your investments. You get taxed on the interest income, dividends, and capital gains received from your investments. However, these monies are not taxed the same way. As a result, they affect the way you manage your portfolio for tax efficiency purposes.

The final chapter delves into the barriers that could block beginner investors from successful investing. One of the major barriers is emptions, especially fear and greed. You may have heard about the *fear of missing out (FOMO)*. Unless you learn how to handle them, you will be unlikely to attain your investment objectives. For example, you might do too many transactions and accrue excessive costs which, in turn, would affect the rate at which your portfolio will grow. So, I provide ways to eliminate emotional investing, such as dollar-cost averaging and learning how to handle losses. Don't feel overwhelmed – I will explain these in detail.

This book will enable you start your journey towards building and maintaining a successful investment portfolio. This works, and has been proven time and time again. For example, a 19-year old student started by gradually saving a total of $1,000 from his campus job. He invested all of it in stocks, and also continued buying more stocks as time went on. Once his money grew by $3,000, he opened a Vanguard brokerage account. After that, he did not look back until his investment grew to $1 million.

So, if you would like to begin this journey to financial freedom, you should start investing now. Begin by reading The Beginner Investor's Guide: Stocks, Cryptocurrencies, Bonds, ETFs, and more now.

CHAPTER 1: INVESTMENT INSTRUMENTS (STOCKS, BONDS, AND MORE)

Most people have incomes from jobs in form of salaries, commissions, and/or bonuses. There is just one problem with this model of generating income. It is difficult to scale and this limits the amount of income you can make. Although it is a common way of making money, a job can also prove to be a pain in the neck. You may find yourself doing a job that you don't like or working for a company that cares little about its employees, or you may also enjoy your job but would like to have more than one stream of income. The good thing is that there are other ways to generate money. All you require to begin is taking a portion of your salary or some of your business income and investing it. You don't need to have a lot of money to start investing. In fact, you can put aside a small amount ($50, $100, or more) for investing on a monthly basis—it will not require as much time as your job to generate the same amount. So, what are the ways you can invest your money?

There are several investment instruments you can put your money in to make more and in this book, and whichever instrument you choose, you will discover how to make the best use of them. Therefore, it requires some basic knowledge to become a good investor. In this chapter, I'll introduce you to some of the investment vehicles you can use to multiply your money. These include stocks, bonds, exchange-traded funds (ETFs), and cryptocurrencies. You may need each to create an investment portfolio that meets your needs and knowing the differences between these instruments will help you. Let's go over each of these instruments, and we begin with stocks.

What Are Stocks?

Stocks can be a great way of building wealth over a period of time. However, it can be an emotional roller coaster ride because they rise and fall in response to shifting market conditions. The more you understand what you're doing, the closer you are to achieving your investment goals. Note that every investors return will be dependent on the amount of risk they are willing to bear hence, results will vary. A stock is part-ownership in a publicly-listed company. For example, if you buy 5,000 shares in a company that has one million shares, you have 0.5% ownership in the business. Stock ownership provides an investor with the chance to make more money as the stock price rises or when the company declares and pays out dividends. There is no guarantee that a company will pay dividends. However, some publicly-listed companies declare dividends monthly, quarterly, or annually, and pay them to qualifying stockholders. As you can see, dividends can be a good source of passive income. There are investors who buy stocks just to earn dividends. Of course, this approach depends on the investor's investment strategy.

Companies use stocks to raise money to fund their business growth projects. There are two broad kinds of stocks in which you may invest: common and preferred stocks. Common stocks offer an investor an opportunity to have a share in a company's profits and losses. Furthermore, a common stockholder has voting rights. In contrast, a preferred stockholder is entitled to a predetermined dividend and has no voting rights. In this book, the word 'stock' refers to common stocks unless expressly stated otherwise.

To make money in stocks, you should buy at a low price and sell at a higher price. Typically, this involves holding the stock for some time to allow the price to appreciate. There can be too much volatility over the short-term to make meaningful returns. Volatility refers to the rate of movement of the stock price. If you want to make money over the short-term, you may want to become a trader instead of an investor. As a result, you need to do some detailed research, analysis and, thorough homework prior to selecting stocks to invest in. Often, such stocks would be for companies with excellent growth prospects and good earnings, such as Amazon, Apple, and Walmart.

If you had invested in Apple in 2012 at the opening price of $12.459 and sold at its 2020 closing price of $132.492, you would have made a return of 963.42%. This means that an investment of $1,000 in Apple would have netted you about $9,634.20. This is way above the basic average stock return of 10%. This confirms that if you invest in a good company, there is money to be made. Coupling the income from the appreciation of the stock with reinvesting the dividends can pump up your investment returns.

We'll talk more about stocks as we proceed with this book. Let me turn my attention to the next investment instrument called cryptocurrencies.

The Basics of Cryptocurrencies

Merriam-Webster defines the prefix crypto as "not openly avowed or declared—often used in combination." That gives you an idea about cryptocurrencies. In short, a cryptocurrency is a digital currency that's based on blockchain technology. A Blockchain is a digital record of transactions, where individual records, called blocks, are linked together in a single list, called a chain. Blockchains are used for recording transactions made with cryptocurrencies. The creators of these digital currencies use blockchain technology to allow decentralization, transparency, and immutability. An outstanding feature of cryptocurrencies is that they are not under the control, regulation, or authority of any individual, government, or agency. Therefore, they cannot be interfered with like *fiat* currencies, such as the U.S. dollar, Canadian dollar, pound sterling, and the Japanese yen. In the 80s and 90s, information technology and software engineers began to create systems to run digital currencies. David Chaum, an American cryptographer, was the first person to produce a digital currency through a Netherland's founded business called DigiCash. Unfortunately, DigiCash finally folded due to its lack of adoption as a currency. The turning point came in 2018 when an anonymous developer called Satoshi Nakamoto produced a peer-to-peer electronic payment system called Bitcoin. The system, although it had flaws, spawned many other cryptocurrencies. Some people erroneously think that a cryptocurrency based on blockchain technology may suffer from double-spending. In theory, it is possible to double spend. In practice, the amount of resources - human, technology, and energy required to enable someone to double-spend renders the feat highly unlikely. It is far easier to *mine* Bitcoin, for example, than to double-spend.

At the time of writing this book, there are over 4,000 cryptocurrencies. The most popular of these currencies is Bitcoin, followed by Ethereum, Litecoin, and Monero. For the first time in its young life, Bitcoin hit the $1 trillion market capitalization mark when it hit a price of nearly $53,000 (Godfrey, 2021). The rest of the cryptocurrencies make less than half of the market capitalization of the first viable digital currency to ever find application by many retailers and consumers (CoinMarketCap, n.d.).

Cryptocurrencies have two major setbacks. They are highly volatile and prone to theft, especially if kept online. To keep them safer, it is better to hold them in offline wallets. Because of extreme volatility, it is advisable to educate yourself before investing in them. However, the good news is you can still make money in cryptocurrencies. Let me illustrate. Suppose you had invested $1,000 in Bitcoin in 2010 when each coin set you back a mere eight cents. That would have pocketed you 80 bitcoins. Fast forward to 2020, just 10 years later, and you would have made a paper profit of nearly $1.83 million on December 16, 2020 when Bitcoin closed at $23,000. That's an incredible return on investment, isn't it? However, you would have obtained such a return at the expense of high volatility, such as the rise and fall that started late in 2017 to 2018.

Despite the volatility of cryptocurrencies, the block technology upon which they are based is growing by leaps and bounds and finding application in many fields. This helps to strengthen the adoption of cryptocurrencies as alternative currencies and assets. Major companies like PayPal and Square have begun to allow users to buy and sell these currencies on their platforms and these developments can only strengthen the adoption of the cryptocurrencies. Like all investment instruments, it is risky to invest in cryptocurrencies because you can lose money. Your best inoculation from the risk is doing your homework to ensure healthy diversification before making any investment. Another important thing about cryptocurrencies: Unlike fiat currencies that are inflationary, cryptocurrencies are deflationary. This means that as long as there is a limited supply of cryptocurrencies like bitcoin, their value should increase. We will now change gears and discuss the next class of investment instruments called bonds.

The Fundamentals of Bonds

Bonds are one of the most common investment vehicles. They are especially useful for the protection of money because they are less risky relative to stocks and cryptocurrencies. What are bonds? A bond is a promise that a company or government extends to you for providing them with the money they need. Why would these entities need this money? Like with stocks, companies need capital to pursue their business goals. A government's needs often involve accomplishing projects that enables the country to function as best as possible. For example, they may raise the money to build roads to allow for commerce to flourish.

You don't just give the company or government money as if it's a gift. You buy their bond. So, a bond is debt security. In return, you'll get back your money coupled with interest. One good example of a bond is the U.S. Savings Bond. You may decide to loan the U.S. government a certain amount, say $1,000. The government exchanges your cash with the bond. You hold this bond until maturity when you liquidate it. The government will give back your money, and the initial money you get is called the face value of a bond. Company and municipal bonds work the same way as the government bonds.

Depending on the type of bond, it is possible to earn a good interest that can range from 4% to 6% (Dogen, 2019). That's the historical bond return from 1926. What does this mean in simple terms? Suppose that you have bought a 10-year bond with a $5,000 face value and a 4% interest. Since bonds often payout interest semi-annually, each of your payments would be worth $100. So far, investing in bonds can generate money for you through interest. However, there's a second way. Instead of holding the security until its maturity date, you may sell the bond when you spot the right opportunity. For example, let us say that you bought $15,000 worth of bonds at their face value. As time goes by, you realize that the value of your bonds is now at $17,500. You may decide to sell at this price and generate $2,500 before costs. The value of bonds increases for two reasons. The borrower's credit profile may improve, resulting in more demand for their bonds. Secondly, the interest rate of newly-issued bonds may decline which increases the interest rates and value of older bonds.

Now, how do you buy bonds? It is easy to buy bonds because they are traded over the counter. However, you need to have a broker to purchase them. We'll talk about how to trade them. Not all bonds are traded over the counter. U.S. Treasury bonds need no middleman or broker as you can buy them directly from the U.S. government. Unlike with stocks, it can be difficult to determine the fair market value of bonds because of the way they are traded. However, the Financial Industry Regulatory Authority (FINRA) keeps an eye on the bond market and helps to maintain fair prices. Like all other financial assets, bonds have risks. The two main risks in the bond market are changing interest rates and defaulting. It is possible for the government, municipal authority, or company to default due to unforeseen circumstances. As a result, you need to do proper research when selecting the type of bonds to add to your investment portfolio. I am not in any way suggesting that you should have bonds in your portfolio. Whether you add them or not depends on your investment goals and risk tolerance level. If you want a high-growth portfolio, you may not need to add bonds or include them as a small percentage. We now move over to the next investment vehicle, called exchange-traded funds.

Basic Knowledge of Exchange-Traded Funds (ETFs)

Exchange-traded funds are investment instruments that can be traded like stocks at an exchange. This means that you can buy and sell them on the New York Stock Exchange, Toronto Stock Exchange and others. ETFs differ from other assets in that they provide diversity without the investor having to select individual securities. A good example of an ETF is the Standard and Poor's (S&P) 500 index ETF, of which there are different types designed for different investment goals. It gives you exposure to the 500 biggest companies listed on the New York Stock Exchange (NYSE) and NASDAQ, all from buying a single ETF share. Building a portfolio of good stocks can be a hard task. That's where ETFs come in and simplify the diversification process.

Various Types of ETFs

ETFs are available in broad categories. For example, there are ETFs in stocks, real estate, commodities and money markets. Currency ETFs are for investing in currencies, such as the U.S. dollar, Euro, or British pound. If investing directly on bonds doesn't attract you and you still want their exposure, you can buy bond ETFs. If you want to invest in commodities like gold and you feel the prices are steep, you may opt to buy commodity ETFs. You can think of as many financial assets as you like and you're likely to find an ETF attached to them. As a beginner, it can be confusing to choose the ETFs you want because there are so many options available. I'll guide you on how to choose the right ETF in the next chapter.

Diversification is one of the most important aspects to consider in your investment strategy. ETFs offer a great asset for this purpose. There are ETFs that *track* the performance of major indexes such as the S&P 500 or the NASDAQ 100. When the index rises by 0.5%, these ETFs also rise by that amount. In contrast, if the index drops by 2%, the said ETFs follow suit by the same amount.

You may be wondering what typical returns you can get from investing in ETFs. Let me answer the question with reference to the S&P 500 index ETF. The return from this ETF from 2000 to 2020 was 5.9% when adjusted for inflation (Best, 2020). This means that if you had invested $10,000 in the ETF over that 10-year period, it would have grown to $31,200 assuming you re-invested the dividends. This isn't a bad return compared to letting your money sit in a conventional savings account.

If there's a downside to investing in ETFs, it is that you don't own the underlying assets. On the positive side, ETFs are a low cost, low volatility (depending on the ETF type), highly liquid, and tax efficient financial asset. However, ETFs can be risky and therefore you should do thorough research in your selection process. Avoid investing in ETFs whose trading volumes are low because, depending on your needs, they may not be as liquid as you want. We have now covered four different assets in which you can invest. There are several more. I would like to discuss mutual funds because they are some of the most common investments and are somewhat relatively safe.

The Basics of Mutual Funds

A mutual fund is a pool of investment money sourced from various investors and companies. It is one of the popular ways of investing, especially for beginners. The fund hires a manager who researches and selects assets in which to invest.

This group or individual focuses on the fund to improve the chances of making respectable returns. When you invest in the fund, you own a portion of it like you do with stocks. Therefore, your share will increase when the fund performs well or decline when it doesn't.

There are two types of mutual funds, namely, *open-ended* and *close-ended*. An open-ended mutual fund is not limited to the total number of shares it issues. This means that shares can be created or destroyed as and when necessary. In contrast, open-ended mutual funds have a fixed number of shares that are often established at the initial public offering (IPO). Consequently, these types of funds' performances are governed by the immutable law of supply and demand.

Why would you consider investing in mutual funds? The fund manager consistently supervises the performance of the fund. This means that there is no need for you to spend a chunk of your time studying financial statements, business models, and calculating the needed financial ratios to select assets. It is essentially a hands-off approach to investing. There are thousands of mutual funds in the U.S. and all over the world from which to choose. What you select will depend on your investment needs. Notice, however, that most funds fail to beat the stock market index, such as the S&P 500. Every fund follows a specific investing strategy. For example, some pools invest expressly in blue-chip business, while others may target the real estate sector. In general, each fund has a set initial minimum investment that starts from around $25 and goes as high as $100,000, plus a fee - typically known as a mutual fund expense ratio or advisor fees.

What returns could you expect from mutual funds? The performance of mutual funds differs from fund to fund. Over a 15-year term, the U.S. large-cap stock funds have returned an average of 8.66% annually or 5.66% when adjusted for inflation. In contrast, 15-year bonds have brought investors around 5.27% inflation unadjusted yearly (Thune, 2020). So, if you had invested $10,000 in the large-cap stocks mutual fund 15 years ago, you would have made $34,757.26.

It is important to note that mutual funds trade differently. They trade only once per day, after the stock markets close. If you enter a trade to buy or sell shares of a mutual fund, your trade will be executed at the next available net asset value (NAV), which is typically calculated after the market closes. This price may be higher or lower than the previous day's closing NAV.

We will look at how to select stocks, bonds, cryptocurrencies, and ETFs shortly. First, let's go through the process of opening a brokerage account.

How to Open a Brokerage Account

Most investors own a brokerage account because it allows for convenient investing. There are several types of brokerage accounts so it may be difficult to choose the right one. You may have heard about some of them like Robinhood, Webull, Qtrade, Questrade, WealthSimple, TD Ameritrade, Fidelity, Charles Swab etc. This section takes you through a step-by-step process to simply your choices. Let's get started.

Select the Type of Brokerage Account

You Need The type of brokerage account that you need depends on your investment objectives. For retirement, the individual retirement account (IRA) is the best account to use in places like the U.S. The traditional IRAs qualify you for tax deductions. However, you cannot access and use your money before you reach 59 and 1/2 years of age. In contrast, the Roth IRA offers no tax benefits. Its advantage is that you qualify for tax-free withdrawals. However, you can only withdraw the contributions you make but you cannot pull out the investment profits. If you are self-employed, you have options such as the SIMPLE IRA, SEP-IRA, or individual 401(k). Of course, these accounts are specific to the United States. If you are resident in Canada, The United Kingdom or other countries, there are typically similar accounts with different names. In Canada, there is the Tax-Free Savings Account (TFSA) and Registered Retirement Savings Plan (RRSP), and in the United Kingdom - the Individual Savings Account (ISA).

If you want to invest for short-term cash needs or for emergencies, then a traditional brokerage account is the appropriate choice. There are no tax advantages because you are taxed on the investment profits and dividends. The big advantage is that you can withdraw money when you want. Hence, this type of account is often called the taxable brokerage account. You have a choice between a cash or margin account. The latter allows you to borrow money to buy assets with the same as collateral. You pay back the money with interest. For a beginner investor, I would try to avoid a margin account until you understand all the dynamics of investing and trading.

Compare Broker Costs, Incentives, and Services

Costs form an important element of investing performance. So, you need to obtain each brokerage firm's pricing schedule and do a detailed comparison. Be aware that investment vehicles like mutual funds, options, ETFs, and bonds may attract their own costs.

Do not be swayed by the incentives that some of these firms offer when you are looking for your brokerage of choice. You may choose an expensive brokerage firm over the long-term. However, there are other factors that may be considered besides costs. So, price should not be the determining factor. You should carefully consider the services and conveniences that each brokerage firm offers. You may find such services valuable because they include access to research reports, detailed historical information, stock picks, trading platforms, foreign trading, fractional shares (buying a part of a share), and other features. So, check the website and features of each firm you're considering.

Select the Right Firm for You

Once you have completed your research, your next step is to choose the firm that best meets your needs. It is simple to open a brokerage account. Head over to the firm's website and fill in the account application. The firm will need your identification such as Social Security number, Social Insurance number, other government identification number, or driver's license. You'll also know other requirements by checking on the firm's website.

Fund the Account

The next step is to fund your brokerage account. Without funds, you cannot buy investments. There are several allowable ways of funding your account, including electronic funds transfer (EFT) and wire transfers. Once you have funds in the account, you are ready to buy the assets that meet your investment objectives. Note that you can fund your brokerage account according to your investment goals - either gradually on a weekly, bi-weekly, monthly, quarterly, annual basis, or an occasional lump sum transfer. Whichever mode you choose, should be determined based on your personal situation.

CHAPTER 2: HOW TO RESEARCH AND PICK SECURITIES FOR YOUR PORTFOLIO

Every investor has their reason(s) for investing and so should you - the reason, or reasons for investing will form your investment goals. Truly, you cannot put your money in the stock market just for fun. Unfortunately, beginner investors often do not give enough thought to the reasons they want to invest their hard-earned cash. This mistake is one of the big reasons for selecting the wrong assets. It follows that, if you want to improve your chances of growing your investment portfolio, you should first work out investment goals or objectives.

Investment Goals and Risk Tolerance

The subject of goals is an important aspect of investing. Goals often enforce accountability, discipline, and motivation to take the necessary steps to achieve them. Without goals, there is absolutely no reason to do anything. People invest their money for various reasons. Fundamentally, all investors want to grow their money without having to work a job.

Some of the main reasons for investing include for retirement, to handle emergencies, for school fees, to start a business, or to buy investment properties. The exact reasons will differ from one investor to the next. Whatever goals you have in mind, they'll fall in the short, medium, or long-term needs of your life.

Effective goals should be specific, measurable, achievable, realistic, and time-based. This strategy of setting goals is called *SMART*, an acronym built from the first letters of the qualities of effective goals. For example, you should state the reason for investing, such as for retirement, and know how much money you want. Furthermore, your goal should be achievable and realistic based on what's possible. You cannot expect a 50% return from investment in the stock market because history says otherwise.

The majority of mutual funds, with dedicated managers, fail to beat the stock market. The same goes for individual investors who manage their own portfolios. According to Gainsglobal, as at June 30, 2020, only 12.8% of U.S. equity managers outperformed the S&P 500 over a 15-year period. Also, you need to spell out when you would want to have the retirement money. Your goals feed into figuring out your risk tolerance. *Risk tolerance* tells you about the amount of risk an investor is willing to assume to achieve their target return. It's a vital concept because it helps you to adopt an appropriate asset allocation and diversification strategy. We'll get to these two concepts shortly because they are central to investor performance. The factors that help to determine an investor's risk tolerance include your age and investment goals. Do not fall in the trap of following conventional wisdom that suggests younger investors can take more risk while older individuals are risk-averse. This idea may be true in some cases, but it is not to be taken as gospel. We are living longer than we used to so older investors don't have to shift their portfolios to include more conservative investments, such as bonds. Money may run out before they depart this planet, and they may face hard financial times.

Other factors that determine investor risk tolerance include your net worth, available risk capital, personal life events, and your investing experience. Net worth measures the difference between the value of your assets (what you own) and liabilities (what you owe).

Risk capital is the amount of money that you are willing to invest without affecting your lifestyle. It is often called disposable income. The more disposable income you have, the more risk you may be willing to take. However, you should not ignore the odds because these often don't change. If there is a two to one chance of losing in an investment, respect it and invest accordingly. The odds don't change because you have more money to invest.

As a beginner investor, you are still in the learning phase. You should be careful with taking large investment risks as your lack of experience could result in significant losses. Start small and take lesser risks to allow for mistakes, and the ability to bounce back and keep going.

How to Allocate Investment Funds

Investing requires money. Therefore, your starting point should be to save. You don't need a lot of money to invest. Put regular (recurring) savings into a brokerage account at whatever level you're comfortable with. It can be as little as from $50 to $500 on a weekly, biweekly, or monthly basis depending on your income and investment goals. Here's how to figure out how much you can save.

- Calculate how much you earn per month after tax.
- Split your spending into essentials (living, mortgage, rent, food, and bills) and non-essentials (movies and entertainment). It is extremely important to pay off any high-interest loans BEFORE investing. The reason for this is any potential interest you make from the stock

market will be erased by any high-interest loans you have.

- Subtract essentials from your total earnings. Decide how much you are willing to add to your portfolio from the remainder.

Avoid taking a personal loan for the purpose of investing in the stock market. If you need the money back in the short-term, like 3–12 months, it will be advisable to keep that money in a high-yield savings account rather than the stock market. The reasoning here is that there is uncertainty in the stock market, which is typically higher in the short-term. For example, the pandemic of 2020 caused the stock market to plunge by more than 40% and rebounded to an all-time high within a few months. Imagine if an investor had immediate plans for the invested funds during that plunge.

The process of allocating funds in various investment assets is called asset allocation. You mix the asset classes, such as bonds, cash, stocks, and real estate, to achieve a certain investment objective. The aim of asset allocation is to minimize risk while simultaneously improving the chances of getting your target return. To do this task effectively requires a knowledge of the risk associated with the different assets that are available in the market.

Equities offer high returns but have a higher risk because they are more volatile. Within the equities, there are large-cap assets that offer the lowest returns but are safer. Small-cap equities typically have high volatility and, therefore, are riskier. As such, you need to find a sweet spot where the risk and return are favorable to you.

Treasury bonds, in contrast, deliver lower returns corresponding with a lower risk. You would not invest wholly in bonds if you wanted to grow your portfolio quicker. That's why we mix assets to create a blend that's likely to help reach the targeted investment objectives. The general theory is that, as you grow older, you should reduce risk so that you can retire while still having sufficient cash to give you a reasonable income.

There are model portfolios available to simplify asset allocation. These models consider both the investment objectives and the risk tolerance of the investor. You still need to tailor them to your own situation. The model portfolios range from conservative to aggressive.

Let's discuss both.

A Conservative Portfolio

A conservative portfolio consists of a high percentage of assets with lower risk, such as money markets. The goal is to protect the principal value of the investment portfolio. For this reason, this portfolio is often called the capital preservation portfolio. A typical conservative portfolio distributes funds in the following way:

- About 70% to 75% consists of fixed income securities;
- Equities make up between 15% and 20%; and
- Highly liquid assets (cash and cash equivalents) contribute 5% to 15% to the fund.

An Aggressive Portfolio

The aggressive portfolio is the opposite of the conservative portfolio. It consists of a high proportion of equities. Because of this, the value of the portfolio tends to fluctuate widely, in some cases, even day-to-day. The aim of the fund is to grow your capital for the long-term. A typical aggressive portfolio has the following mix of assets:

- Fixed-income securities add up to between 20% and 25%;
- Cash and cash equivalents contribute between 5% and 10% to the portfolio; and
- Equities make up to between 50% and 55%.

There is another portfolio that's more aggressive and consists of over 80% in equities. Notice that the examples given above are not fixed. You can adjust them to suit your individual investment needs. If liquidity is more important to you, put a large proportion of your portfolio in short-term fixed income securities. For a high risk-tolerant investor with no need for high liquidity, cash and cash equivalents should make up a smaller part of the portfolio. Having given enough thought to your investment goals, risk tolerance, and choice of a portfolio, you are ready to begin looking for the right assets. One of the major assets that make up most portfolios is stocks.

How to Value a Stock

The key decision to make when selecting stocks from your portfolio is their value. You don't want to buy an overpriced stock because you can lose money almost immediately. So, you need to value the stock. The process of valuing stocks is called stock valuation. The big idea is to figure out the intrinsic value ('true' value) of the stock. This value is not necessarily the same as the stock's current market price.

Knowing the intrinsic value of a stock allows you to determine whether the stock is overpriced or undervalued. An undervalued stock sells at a discount. Buying such a stock is like buying a car or property at below its market price. You can turn around and sell it at its market price and make a profit. Ideally, you want to always invest in the stocks that are undervalued.

There are valuation methods that can help you to figure out the intrinsic values of stocks. It may not be easy to choose the best method because of the large number available. Some of these methods are simple to use while others are more complicated. There is no single method that's applicable to all stocks and industries. At times, you may have to use more than one method to value your target stock. Let's get deeper into these valuation methods.

The Two Categories of Valuation Methods
Valuation methods fall into two categories, *absolute* and *relative* valuation. Let's briefly look at each of these methods.

Absolute Valuation
This method of valuation is used to figure out the intrinsic value of an investment by using the fundamentals of the company in isolation without any comparison with its competitors or similar companies. This valuation method is somewhat problematic because it ignores competitive analysis, which is important to understand the business or industry. The key fundamentals considered include *cash flow* and *dividends*. This approach requires some level of understanding of financial statements and reporting assumptions as it relies heavily on reported financial data. Models using absolute valuation include the discounted dividend model, discounted cash flow model, discounted residual income model, and the discounted asset-based model.

Relative Valuation
Unlike the absolute valuation method, here, an asset is compared with other similar assets. For example, a stock in the technology industry is compared with another in the same sector. This method involves determining multiples and ratios, such as the price-to-earnings (P/E) ratio, and comparing them to those of similar companies. A company with a higher P/E ratio than a similar business may be seen as being overvalued. It is faster and easier to use the absolute valuation method. However, beginner investors often prefer the relative valuation method for its simplicity or rely on the valuation tools and information provided by their brokerages.

Let's go over three popular valuation models.

The Discounted Dividend Model (DDM)

The discounted dividend model (DDM) is an absolute valuation approach, which uses the dividends a company pays out to calculate the intrinsic value of the stock. Dividends represent the actual cash flowing to stockholders. The present value of these cash flows provide a way to value the stock.

To use the method, the first thing you do is to determine if the company pays a dividend. A good resource for this is Yahoo Finance. Once done, you establish if the dividend is regular and predictable. Such dividends are more likely to be found on blue-chip companies. The way you check for dividend payout predictability is by computing the increase from one year to the next.

Suppose imaginary company PQR pays dividends as per schedule shown below:

	2014	2015	2016	2017	2018	2019
Dividend per share ($)	0.45	0.49	0.52	0.56	0.60	0.63
% Change	-	8.89%	6.12%	7.69%	7.14%	5.00%

% Change = (0.49-0.45)/0.45 x 100 = 8.89%

On average, from 2014 to 2019, the company increased its dividend payment by around 6.97%. Importantly, the company paid the dividend annually. So, you could expect it to do so again in future years unless they change their policy or experience a business event that affects its ability to make profits. To improve your confidence in the analysis, you could also determine the increase in company earnings from year to year to identify the trend in relation to dividend payouts. If your brokerage account provides this information, it can save you a lot of time.

The Discounted Cash Flow (DCF) Model

Sometimes the DDM is not applicable due to irregular dividend payouts or the company doesn't pay any dividend. How do you value a stock in these situations? You use the discounted cash flow (DCF) model. This approach uses the business's discounted future cash flows to assess the company's stock value. This model is suitable for any company, whether paying a dividend or not.

The DCF works only if your target company shows *stable*, *positive*, and *predictable* cash flows. Note that cash flow is the net amount of cash and cash-equivalents transferred into and out of a business. A company's ability to create value is determined by its ability to generate positive cash flows.

The Discounted Residual Income Model

The discounted residual income model considers all expected cash flows after payment to suppliers and other external parties. This residual amount is then discounted to arrive at the valuation of the company. It is important to note that payments due to bondholders and preference shareholders are not subtracted from the total.

The Discounted Asset Model

The discounted asset model is based on the premise that a business is equal to the sum of its parts. This model values a company based on the market value of its owned assets. It is calculated by looking at the present value of each asset, and adding them up to arrive at the total asset value. This method is somewhat objective and does not entirely rely on subjective judgement.

The Comparables Model

The comparables model is a relative valuation approach that is often used when investors and analysts want to compare stocks with benchmarks. What investors do is compare a stock's price multiples against a benchmark to figure out if the stock is underpriced or overvalued. The model depends on the idea that similar assets should be valued equally.

There are several ratios or multiples that can be used including the price-to-earnings (P/E), price-to-book (P/B), price-to-sales (P/S), and price-to-cash (P/C) ratios. A ratio, by the way, is the outcome you get after dividing two numbers. For example, dividing $40 by $10 gives an answer of 4. In other words, the ratio is 4:1. The most common ratio is the P/E because it tells the investor about the earnings of the company, which is one of the most important metrics that drives the value of an investment. It works well for publicly-traded companies because an investor can access the stock's price and the company's earnings. However, for the ratio to work, the earnings should be strong and not be too volatile.

Using Fundamental and Technical Analysis

The valuation methods we discussed in the previous section are a part of a strategy used to select stocks called fundamental analysis. The second approach to choosing investment assets is called technical analysis. The former is the main tool used by long-term investors while the latter finds favor with traders. As an investor, you should become familiar with these two approaches because they serve different, but important purposes. A lot of investors also use both approaches. Let's begin with understanding the basics of fundamental analysis.

Fundamental Analysis

Fundamental analysis deals with evaluating a company's performance to determine its financial health. There are several factors to look at that are both internal and external of the business. Looking at the financial statements in isolation is not sufficient to understand a company and its business climate. It is also vital to understand its management and business model. When done with your analysis, you should be able to establish if the company's stock is below or above its prevailing market price.

The workhorses of fundamental analysis are the company's financial statements. The first tool you analyze are the earnings statements. The purpose of this analysis is to determine the amount of money the business has made in the past and whether that value is declining or growing. A business whose earnings and profit grow often results in higher stock prices and dividends, if any.

There are financial ratios that give investors an idea whether the business's financial situation is healthy or not. Many resources offer the information you need to perform fundamental analysis on any company that's listed on a stock exchange. One of the skills you'll need to have is to read financial statements. The most common resources include *Yahoo Finance*, *Tipranks.com*, and *Google Finance*. This means that you don't have to calculate some of the financial ratios because you'll find them on these resources. Let me take you through some of the most important ratios you'll need when you do your fundamental analysis.

Important Financial Ratios

Financial ratios are divided into four categories - the profitability, liquidity, solvency, and valuation ratios. Their purpose is to provide you with insight into the companies that you are considering investing in. Let us go over each category of ratios for a better understanding.

The Profitability Ratios

There is nothing that an investor cares more about in a company than its profitability. How profitable a business is gives an idea about the earnings the investors could potentially receive in the form of dividends. The profitability ratios reveal this information. Furthermore, they make it easy to choose certain stocks as opposed to others. A company may be turning over a lot of money in revenue but the real question is - are they making any profit? In other words, after all the operating and non-operating costs are deducted from the revenue, is there any of that revenue left?

Profitability ratios include metrics such as the operating margin, return on equity (ROE), and return on investment (ROI). Of these ratios, the net profit margin receives more attention because it tells the investor how much of the revenue becomes profit or net income. Here's how to calculate the operating margin:

Net Profit Margin = (Net Income/Revenue) x 100

It is easy to compare your target stock against similar others and the industry. A low net profit margin is a sign that the market conditions are not favorable, competition tougher, or weaker cost control (or rising costs). There could be a host of other reasons so it is advisable to consider other business factors as well.

Liquidity Ratios

Liquidity ratios measure how quickly the company can turn its assets into cash to repay its debts. In other words, these ratios give an indication of operational efficiency. Typical ratios include *cash ratio, current ratio, inventory turnover*, and *quick ratio*. Of these, the quick and current ratios are the most common.

By definition, the current ratio is obtained by dividing current assets by current liabilities. In formula form, you calculate the current ratio like this:

Current ratio = (Current Assets/Liabilities)

Current assets and liabilities represent 12-months' worth of business activities. A high ratio means that current assets are more than enough to cover the cost of current liabilities.

The quick ratio, usually called the Acid-test ratio, is a variation of the current ratio that excludes inventory from the current assets. This ratio includes only assets that can be converted to cash within 90 days or less.

Quick ratio = (Current assets - Inventory)/Current Liabilities

The higher the quick ratio, the better as this indicates that the business is sufficiently liquid to fulfill its short-term liabilities.

Solvency Ratios

The solvency ratios determine the ability of a business to handle its long-term debt. A business with large, future financial obligations rarely finds favor with investors compared to a company with a lower debt. Some of the common ratios include net income to liabilities, debt to equity, and debt to total assets. Investors prefer to use debt to assets and debt to equity ratios for establishing a business's solvency position. Let's look deeper into the debt to total assets ratio and how investors calculate it.

By definition, debt to total assets ratio compares the total amount of debt a business has to its total assets. Here is the formula to use to calculate this ratio:

Debt to total assets = (Short term debt + Long term debt)/Total assets

Since total assets are in the denominator, the lower the ratio, the more favorable to a business. It shows that the total assets far outweigh the available debt. Such a company is less risky to invest in because the business would still remain with some assets if creditors demand their money. Like with the other ratios, it is important to compare the debt to total assets ratio of your target company with the industry and other similar types of businesses.

Valuation Ratios

Almost all experienced long-term investors use the valuation ratios to determine the value of a company. They are the most common ratios to assess the attractiveness of a business for investing purposes. With these ratios, you can establish if the prevailing stock price is expensive or relatively cheap. The lower the ratio, the more attractive the company. Some of the common valuation ratios include the price-to-earnings (P/E), price-to-book (P/B), price-to-sales (P/S), and the price-to-cash flow (P/CF).
Let's look deeper into the P/E, the most common valuation ratio.

The P/E is the one of the most popular of all the valuation ratios. Its purpose is to evaluate how a company's stock price compares with its earnings per share (EPS). Furthermore, the P/E ratio tells you the premium investors are willing to pay for the stock. Here's how you calculate it:

P/E ratio = Market or Current Price per share/Earnings per share

The number you get tells you how much buyers are paying for the stock for every $1 of the underlying company's earnings. On its own, the P/E ratio does not add much value. It is only when you compare your target company's P/E with that of the industry and its peers that the ratio means something.

All the ratios we discussed above are part of fundamental analysis. You can undoubtedly realize how important this analysis is to selecting stocks and other securities like corporate bonds. You would not want to buy a bond offered by a company that can easily default, would you? Surely not.

The question that beginner investors often ask is around the timing of buying an asset. Fundamental analysis is limited when it comes to answering this question. As long as the market price is below the intrinsic value, you can buy. However, you can maximize your returns by buying at the most favorable price. This is where technical analysis comes in - let's delve in.

Technical Analysis
Technical analysis is a tool favored more by traders than investors because they rely heavily on timing their entry and exit from the market. No one said long-term investors should not use it. It can supplement the already useful fundamental analysis. Technical analysis is the study of price movements and volumes of transactions to time entry and exit from the market.

This discipline uses charts or graphs that show past price movements and volumes. The patterns identified, coupled with signals, help to forecast future movements. Based on this information, you can decide the right time to enter or sell your asset. The most common charts for this purpose include the linear, bar, and candlestick charts. As such, the foundation of learning technical analysis is to study these charts and signals such as moving averages and oscillators. I won't go into the details of these charts because they are beyond the scope of this book however, if you are interested in knowing more about this, a good resource is *investopedia.com* and you can see some real-life charts on *Yahoo Finance.*

It is advisable to use both the fundamental and technical analyses to attain a full picture of an asset and be well-positioned to buy or sell it at the right time to achieve your investment goals.

One of the vital processes to consider when building an investment portfolio is proper diversification. Let's discuss this.

Diversifying Your Investment Portfolio

Beginning investors often confuse diversification and asset allocation. The latter is a subset of diversification. Asset allocation involves grouping asset classes in different proportions. You can think of it as a high-level form of diversification. The asset classes refer to financial instruments such as stocks, bonds, ETFs, cryptocurrency, and commodities. An example of an asset allocation may be 70% stocks, 10% bonds, 15% cash, and 5% cryptocurrencies.

Diversification, on the other hand, refers to spreading your investments across and within various asset classes. This means that in the 70% stocks of the above portfolio, you may invest in financial, artificial intelligence, and technology stocks. The 10% bonds could include a certain amount of Treasury and corporate bonds. Furthermore, stocks could be diversified to include large-capitalization (large-cap), mid-capitalization (mid-cap), and small-capitalization (small-cap) stocks.

Why diversify? The big idea is to avoid putting all your eggs in one basket. If, for some reason, the basket falls, you could lose all your eggs. However, if your eggs are in different baskets, they will not be exposed to the same factors. You diversify to minimize the risk of losing your capital while getting a reasonable return on your money. The effective approach of diversifying is to buy assets in different classes, industries, market locality, and company sizes. Some assets in your portfolio may face tough times and perform poorly while others may perform well. The overall effect will be to nullify the impact of the poorly performing assets. Now, how do you select the assets you may want in your portfolio? Let us answer this question in the next section.

How to Select Asset Classes for Your Portfolio

You have now decided on your investment goals, risk tolerance, and figured out the right diversification. The next step is to select the actual assets to build the portfolio. Let's begin with choosing stocks.

How to Select a Stock

There is too much information out there that recommends buying certain stocks. This is well and true, but the analysts who produce the stock picks don't risk their money when you buy. It's you who bear the risk. Therefore, you need to take the responsibility to ensure that the recommended stock passes your investment criteria. In other words, depend on yourself as much as possible, even if you are a beginner. You never know what drives these analysts to make certain predictions. Always do your own research even if it may take time. That's where emotional control is paramount. Investing is a rational sport. Therefore, it is important to analyze your target assets before you buy them.

Here's how to go about choosing the right stocks for your portfolio. First, select the sector that you are familiar with. You do this because you'll understand the stocks within it much better and make sound investment decisions. For example, if you work in the health care sector, you may want to begin from that sector.

Once you have selected the industry, go ahead and choose stocks that may perform to your liking. This is where you'll use fundamental analysis and financial ratios. Always compare the stocks with one another and the industry. Ensure that you understand the business, and it serves people with products and services that are in demand and will remain so in the foreseeable future. The stock you decide on must have a competitive edge over its peers. Find out what investors think about the potential stock. A great resource is TiPRanks.com. After completing your fundamental analysis, you should have a stock to invest in. Next, you time your entry by using technical analysis. Be patient and wait for the right time. Again, you have to keep your emotions in check or else you may enter at the wrong time. It is important to avoid chasing the bull. This is typically marked by a steep and somewhat continued rise in the stock price within a relatively short period of time. Some investors buy in without doing any due diligence due to the fear of missing out. Note that when this happens, the reason for the spike in price is already incorporated in the price and buying in after the spike may position you for a loss. It is advisable to wait for a dip in the stock price as there is almost always a dip. That's all it takes to choose the right stock for your portfolio. We now turn to bond selection.

Choosing a Bond for Your Portfolio

You want to buy bonds that pay you a good interest rate and are less risky to possible defaults. That's why you need to consider two major factors when selecting bonds for your portfolio - credit rating of the borrower, and the bond yield.

- **Credit rating:** The borrower behind the bond should have a demonstrable record of paying its bonds. If you buy a bond from an institution with a bad credit rating, you may wind up sitting with a paper that has no value. Credit rating agencies, like Moody's and Standard and Poor's, rate governments and other entities that offer bonds. The highest rating is the AAA (triple A). The U.S. Treasury is considered the Rolls-Royce of bonds because it is the safest and is often used as a benchmark.

- **Bond yield:** This is the return you gain for investing in bonds. You calculate it by dividing the expected amount of interest by the bond face value. Compare between the different bond yields and make your choice. Only look at this factor once you are happy that the entity offering the bond has a high chance of paying it.

How to Select an ETF

There are over 2,000 ETFs listed on exchanges in the U.S. and across the world, the number exceeds 5,000. It can be difficult to choose a few from such large numbers. What you need is an ETF selection criterion that's in line with your investment needs. With that in hand, you may go ahead and choose the fund you need.

The ETF screener, like that of Vanguard and Qtrade, allows for an easy selection. You can find out if your broker offers this feature. It's easy to access an ETF screener by going and searching on your favorite search engine. Once you have access to the screener, select the funds that meet criteria such as the following:

- **Expense ratio:** This is the money charged to manage your portfolio. You want it to be as low as possible.
- **Trading volume:** You want to look out for an ETF that has good volume because this indicates a fund with good liquidity.
- **Size of assets under management:** The higher the value of the assets, the better.
- **Date of inception:** It is a good idea to buy an ETF with a record of good performance. The chances are higher that it may continue to perform well.
- **How the ETF tracks its benchmark:** You should choose an ETF that either matches or outperforms its benchmark.

You can also select between a passively- or actively-traded ETF. The passively-traded ETFs are often better because their counterparts usually trail their benchmarks. Furthermore, the actively-traded ETFs can offer good performance over the long term. If you intend to invest for the short-term, actively-traded ETFs might be the better option.

The final asset to look at is cryptocurrencies.

Choosing a Cryptocurrency to Invest In

There are over 1,500 cryptocurrencies in the digital currency market and many were created in the last five years (BitDegree, 2021). It can be confusing to decide which cryptocurrency offers the best value for your investment. As at March 2021, the cryptocurrency market size is about $1.67 trillion with bitcoin sitting at $1.01 trillion, which is just over 60% of the market.

Although the industry is young compared to others, like commodities and foreign exchange, it has gained popularity largely due to the value of the blockchain technology that drives it. This technology is revolutionizing many industries from finance to law. The weak point of this industry is that it has high volatility so it may be a good idea to invest in cryptocurrencies for the long term.

As with other assets, you need to do your own research to find the right currency to invest in. The following questions will help you in your investigations.

- Does the currency have strong backers that include savvy founders and developers?
- Is the currency solving people-specific problems? Are these problems likely to continue into the future?
- How good is the technology of the currency relative to that of its peers or competitors?
- How sound is the plan of the founders?

Armed with the answers to these questions, you may then decide on the cryptocurrency most likely to deliver the results you desire. Do not allow your emotions run wild when you make investment decisions. Also, be wary of too much noise, especially from people who don't understand the technology that drives your chosen cryptocurrency.

You should be ready to build your portfolio after going through this section. However, investment success does not stop here. There is still the task of managing your portfolio, the subject of our next chapter.

CHAPTER 3: HOW TO MANAGE YOUR PORTFOLIO LIKE A PRO

Successful investing is the product of effective portfolio management. This process begins when you decide to invest right through to reaching your investment goals. In essence, portfolio management is the process of taking the necessary steps to create and maintain an investment portfolio to meet your investment objectives. Underlying the success of portfolio management is the investor's objectives and risk tolerance. The process begins with planning where you specify your investment objectives and work out your risk tolerance. Only then can you build the portfolio geared to attain your investment goals without putting your capital at high risk. This step is called execution. As soon as the portfolio is in place, your next steps include monitoring and evaluation to ensure that you stay on track to reach your investment objectives. Before we look at monitoring and evaluation, there are some things you need to address for portfolio management to be easier.

Important Considerations in Portfolio Management

If it were easy to succeed in investing, everyone would do it by themselves. It is simple, yet not easy to execute because you need to adopt certain behaviors proven to lead to investment success. I'd like to share a few behaviors with you so that you consider adopting them in your portfolio management process.

Reduce Expenses and Fees

Undertaking asset transactions costs money in the form of commissions, fees, and taxes. Frequent trading can substantially increase costs and reduce the amount of money that you make. Over the long term, you may not only lose money, but the opportunity cost as well. In other words, the money you spend on fees and other costs could be used to make more money. Let me illustrate.

Suppose it is 1960, you are 21 years old, and you want to retire at 65. This means that you'd work for 44 years. Furthermore, you are determined so you save money aggressively, and invest $10,000 annually in good small-cap stocks that return 12%. At this rate of return, by the time you retire you would have amassed $6.5 million if you paid only 2% in costs. That's an amount that a lot of investors wouldn't mind. However, what would have happened if most of the 2% went into your investments instead of transaction costs?

You would have made a whopping $12 million, which is nearly double what you got. Can you see the impact of expenses on your wealth? So, pay attention to costs and avoid making frequent transactions. I discuss this in detail in the next section.

Buy Assets That You Understand

Fundamental and technical analyses help in choosing assets to invest in. Investing success depends more on accurate forecast estimates than any ability. You want to know where the business you are researching might go in the foreseeable future. This process can be simplified if you understand the business environment better. Not only should you understand the business, but also the industry it operates in.

If you invest in a business you barely understand, it could lead to frequent transactions as you enter and exit trades more often. Frequent trading is a result of the fear of missing out, and the consequence of investing in businesses you don't understand.

On the contrary, when you invest in a business you understand, you will be relatively comfortable with your position and less likely to panic when there is a market or business event that causes a stock market frenzy. As others panic and sell due to the fear of losing, you will relax and possibly buy more shares to add to your position. Most investors refer to this as *taking advantage of a sale.*

Build a Margin of Safety

Adding a safety margin when you buy is the single most important action you can take to protect your portfolio. There are two ways of doing this.

The first is to make conservative valuations. We have a tendency of becoming too optimistic when times are good. Subsequently, we can make investing mistakes. For example, when growth rates of a business look good, we tend to inflate the future performance of a business. Yet, varying growth rates can bring vastly different profits. A 7% growth rate will bring lower profits than if it is 14%. So, overvaluing a company could cause you to buy beyond the real value of the business. If you are going off the valuation by your broker, you will be better off going with the average or worst-case valuation scenario.

Secondly, try to avoid buying above or at the intrinsic value of a business. The price you pay for an asset determines your rate of return. So, the lower the price you pay, the higher the return on your investment. Therefore, when buying an asset, ensure that you pay near but below the intrinsic value for great businesses. In contrast, pay for well below the intrinsic values for all other good but not-so-great businesses.

Taking the above steps will get you on the right track with managing your investment portfolio. Once you have bought the assets, there are two further steps to take to ensure that your portfolio stays in line to deliver as per your expectations. The first is monitoring and the second is rebalancing. Let's briefly go over monitoring.

Monitoring Your Investment Portfolio

How would you know if your investment portfolio is delivering what you want? You do that by monitoring it. When you realize that it has shifted away from your objectives, you rebalance it as long as your circumstances have not changed. There are many factors that can cause your portfolio to drift from your target. Your needs and circumstances, and the market might change. These are the main things that you need to monitor and you should evaluate how they impact your portfolio.

The changes that can happen in your life are varied. Typical changes may include changes in your employment status, marital situation, and risk preferences. Furthermore, you may need money to spend for whatever reason including in events like divorce, death of a spouse, or a court judgment. Another key factor could be the changes to the law and regulations that affect your assets. When these changes occur, your asset allocation may shift from the proportions you set from the beginning. You need to catch the impact soon to make timely adjustments.

The market and economy could also change and affect your investment portfolio. Factors in this category include market cycles, risk attributes of assets, inflation, and the central bank policy. Usually, these changes could lead to a need for rebalancing of your portfolio. Let's go over how to do this so that you can do it yourself.

Rebalancing Your Asset Allocation

Rebalancing is the process of strategically buying one type of asset and selling another to retain a given asset allocation. This allows you to stay on course to achieve your desired investment objectives. Sometimes, you don't need to buy and sell assets but to add to your already existing allocations.

For example, if your initial risk tolerance and objectives require you to have 80% stocks and 20% bonds in your portfolio, rebalancing should aim at keeping the asset mix unchanged. If the blend changes to 60% stocks and

40% bonds, you can sell a portion of your bonds and buy more stocks to re-establish your initial 80-20 split. Alternatively, you can buy more of the stocks to reduce the bonds. I'll show you how to do this practically.

Why You Should Rebalance Your Portfolio

Informing you that you should rebalance your portfolio is well and good. However, you should understand what an unbalanced portfolio means. Take a look at this example.

Sue had $20,000 to invest. She put $12,000 into stocks, $5,000 in bonds, and $3,000 in cash and cash equivalents. Therefore, the asset allocation she achieved was as follows: 60% stocks, 25% bonds, and 15% cash. She was happy with the allocation. When she learned how to invest, she became aware that she should monitor her portfolio.

After five years of consistent monitoring, Sue realized that her stock proportion had doubled to $24,000, bonds had increased to $6,250, and cash rose to $3,450 (15% of her portfolio). Her portfolio was worth $33,700 when she made these observations. She knew how to check if the portfolio was still balanced.

After doing a little math, she found out that stocks were at 71% ($24,000/$33,700) of the portfolio. Bonds and cash made 19% and 10% of the portfolio, respectively. The new portfolio was heavily reliant on the performance of stocks.

The problem is that stocks are more volatile than bonds and cash, and therefore increase the risk exposure. However, Sue's risk tolerance hadn't changed. Therefore, she had to rebalance her portfolio. Do you now see clearly why rebalancing is necessary? In the next section, we will see how to rebalance an unbalanced portfolio.

How to Rebalance Your Portfolio

The basic premise of rebalancing a portfolio is to sell a portion of your best-performing asset and increase the holding of the lowest-performing securities. All it takes to figure out how to rebalance your portfolio is to do some basic math. Let me illustrate by rebalancing Sue's portfolio that I talked about earlier.

If you recall, the target portfolio should consist of 60% stocks, 25% bonds, and 15% cash. After five years, the portfolio's asset allocation shifted to 71% stocks, 19% bonds, and 15% cash. Furthermore, the portfolio's value sits at $33,700. All it takes is to split this amount into proportions of 60% stocks, 25% bonds, and 15% cash. Here's how you do it.

Compute the needed value of stocks by multiplying the value of the portfolio by 60%, the percentage of stocks you want. Doing so leads to $20,220. Similarly, you'll obtain $8,425 and $5,055 for bonds and cash, respectively. With that completed, you need to figure out how to adjust the current asset values to match the numbers you've just calculated.

The required value of the stock is lower than is available. So, you should sell stocks to the value of $3,780 ($24,000–$20,220), buy bonds worth $2,175 ($8,425–$6,250), and keep cash or cash equivalents of $5,055. Thus, you would have rebalanced Sue's portfolio to an asset allocation profile that is geared towards meeting her investment goals.

There are two problems associated with rebalancing a portfolio in this way. You'll certainly pay transaction fees and may have to pay capital gains tax. We'll deal with taxes in a separate section in this chapter. The transaction costs may not seem much in percentage terms, but they can be huge on a large portfolio. How do you minimize these costs?

You cannot entirely avoid them, but you can reduce their number of transactions. In the example above, you have at least two transactions, selling stocks and buying bonds. There may be another transaction depending on the form of cash in your portfolio.

It is possible to cut the number of transactions to just one - this requires buying more of the lowest-performing asset(s). In our example, Sue would have to buy more bonds and increase her cash amount in her portfolio. The question is, "How many bonds should she buy?"

Her portfolio consists of 60% stocks valued at $24,000. Remember that, after five years, Sue's portfolio had $24,000 worth of stocks, and the new one would have the same amount in these securities. Since we want the proportion of stocks to be 60%, this should be equivalent to $24,000. From this amount, we work out the required value of the new portfolio. We divide the value of stocks ($24,000) by 60% and get $40,000. Now, 25% and 15% of this portfolio should be bonds and cash, respectively. Therefore, the bonds' value should be $10,000 while cash makes up $6,000.

This means that you should add $6,300 to your portfolio and buy additional bonds worth $3,750. The balance of the money ($2,550) will go to cash. After these actions, Sue's portfolio would be rebalanced. I get that not every investor will have this cash lying around somewhere. But if you have it, and the transaction costs exceed the extra money you need to rebalance your portfolio, it makes financial sense to add it to your investment purse. The big advantage with this approach is that you let the best-performing asset continue to make money for you.

This table depicts both rebalancing strategies.

	Stocks	Bonds	Cash and its Equivalents	Total
Initial Portfolio Profile	$12,000 60%	$5,000 25%	$3,000 15%	$20,000 100%
After 5 years	$24,000 71%	$6,250 19%	$3,450 10%	$33,700 100%
Rebalancing Strategy #1	<Sell> $20,220 60%	<Buy> $8,425 25%	<Add> $5,055 15%	$33,700 100%
Rebalancing Strategy #2	No action $24,000 60%	<Buy> $10,000 25%	<Add> $6,000 15%	$40,000 100%

As we discussed rebalancing your portfolio, you be wondering when to do it. Should you do it each time there is a significant change or at set time intervals? Let me provide an answer to that question in the next section.

When to Rebalance Your Portfolio

Investors differ on the timing of rebalancing portfolios. You have a choice of either doing it at regular intervals or at predetermined asset allocation points. Some investors rebalance their portfolios monthly, quarterly, or annually. The problem with this approach is that it isn't flexible.

Rebalancing based on deviations from your target asset allocations is ideal because markets can change any time. The rule of thumb is to adjust your portfolio when assets shift by around 5% (SoFi Learn, 2021). This method is called the *percentage-of-portfolio rebalancing*. It works like this: If you have a portfolio that has 55% domestic stocks, 15% bonds, and 30%, and one of the assets increases by 5%, then you rebalance. You also rebalance if the asset drops by 5%. How often you rebalance your portfolio also may depend on what stage you are in life - someone closer to retirement may want to rebalance more often as a way to reduce risk exposure.

Portfolio Management and Taxes

The subject of tax is crucial for effective portfolio management. It should begin right when you decide which brokerage account to open. Whether you are investing from North America, the UK, or other parts of the world, there are brokerage accounts that are tax advantageous to an investor.

In Canada, you can open a Registered Retirement Savings Plan (RRSP) in which to hold your investments. Its advantage is that it is a tax-sheltered account. This means that you are not taxed as your investments grow within it. You fund it with pre-tax money, then buy investments that meet your criteria. It works well for an investor who holds the investments for the long term, especially until retirement. It is important to note that when you eventually make a withdrawal, you'll be taxed based on your tax bracket at that time. If you defer withdrawals till retirement, assuming you will be earning a lower income at that time, you'll be taxed at a lower rate. This is like using the government's money to grow your investment portfolio. The RRSP works similarly to the traditional IRA of the US. In places like the UK, you can also find accounts called Individual Savings Accounts (ISAs) for stocks and shares. They offer tax-free savings up to certain limits.

There are other accounts, like Canada's Tax-Free Savings Account (TFSA) and the U.S.'s Roth IRA that also provide tax-free advantages. You fund them with after-tax money and therefore, are not taxed when you withdraw. Importantly, you don't get taxed on your earnings growth as well. This is a plus. It's important to choose an account that minimizes the amount of taxes you pay. However, there is more that you should know about taxes. When you invest, you may get different types of investment income, such as interest, dividends, and capital gain. Interest income is the money you get from owning an investment asset like bonds. A dividend is money that certain companies choose to payout to its stockholders. It is a portion of the profit that the company makes over a given operational period.

Capital gains is income from the sale of an asset such as stocks. Some of the stocks you may own may appreciate in value over time. If you sell at these values, you'll keep the difference between the price you paid for the stock and the amount you sold it for. For example, if you buy a share of a given stock $20 and sell it later for $26, the capital gain is $4 ($26 - $24). I excluded commissions in the calculation for simplicity purposes, but not that in a real-world situation, any transaction will incur a fee, which should be deducted from the sale price to arrive at the final gain.

The way these incomes are taxed often differ from one country to the next. In the U.S. and Canada, interest income is taxed at your marginal rate because it is seen as ordinary income. It is the least tax-efficient way of earning investment money. In the UK, interest is tax-free up to £5,000 with the starting rate for savings and up to £1,000 with the Personal Savings Allowance (the Money Advice Service, n.d.).

Capital gains receives the most tax favor because it originates from a company that would already have been taxed. In the U.S., capital gains tax depends on the length of holding the investment and can be 0%, 15%, or 20% based on your taxable income.

In Canada, only 50% of the income is taxed (RBC Global Asset Management, n.d.). You can expect to pay between 10% and 20% capital gains tax if you are in the U.K., depending on your tax bracket (Crunch., 2021). In Canada, dividends get taxed at a lower rate than interest while in the U.S., the tax rate on dividends depends on the location of the paying entity. If the entity is based in the U.S., the dividend attracts 20% tax and when paid by other companies, the rate is the same as the income tax (O'Hara, 2020). For the U.K., the tax rate on the dividend starts from 7.5% to 38.1% in the 2020/2021 tax year (Crunch., 2021).

Important: Ensure that you consult with your tax advisor and do your research to receive the most up-to-date tax information and advice.

As you can see, you need to build your portfolio and manage it with an eye on how taxes can impact it. Before you rebalance, check how best to do it without incurring excessive taxes.

CHAPTER 4: BARRIERS TO BEGINNER INVESTING SUCCESS

The foundation of success in any field whether financial, academic, career, or business is not technical skills. These skills are essential to perform certain functions. However, the quality of a person's performance is a function of their mindset. Most beginner investors usually make emotional decisions or base their investment choices on rumors or some YouTube videos. When someone touts a hot new opportunity, they gravitate to it en masse and without doing proper due diligence. As a result, many lose money and fail to understand why.

It is astonishing why many keep doing this even when they don't get the results they desire. They remind me of entrepreneurs who fail because they don't research their customers. Even after being guided on why and how to know their customers, they continue leaving the step out, and keep failing. I agree that you may fail in the beginning, but you need to review your investment decisions, correct where necessary, and you'll see better performance as time progresses.

There are certain behaviors that you need to deal with before you can succeed in self-directed investing. Although each investor is different, there are certain common barriers every beginner must be aware of. I'll share them with you and offer ways to deal with them.

Making Emotional Investing Decisions

Emotions are so powerful they drive nearly everything that you and I do. We are wired, from birth, for survival. That's why the fight or flight mode is so prevalent in many of our behaviors. When you add the fact that we are social, the effect of emotions is magnified. There are two vital emotions that trouble almost all investors and they are fear and greed. These are so powerful that they overcome most investors' reasoning power if they have an underdeveloped will. Consequently, they make bad decisions that lose them their investing capital. There are ways to train the will, but that will require a separate book.

Every investor knows that they should buy low and sell high. This is fundamental and logical. Yet, investors often panic when prices of assets decline heavily, and they sell even good securities that they should hang onto. Emotions overcome this logic of investing. Strange as it may sound, market participants have a tendency of buying at the top of the market and selling at the bottom due to panic. Money flow analysis of mutual funds historically proves this tendency. Investors who understand human psychology notice these irrational investing behaviors and make huge profits as a result. This is not a new thing.

Jesse Livermore and Richard Wyckoff, both savvy traders in the early 20th century, have written about this behavior. Wyckoff developed a five-step approach that helped traders and investors to take advantage of this human behavior. He showed through technical analysis that most investors panic and sell their stocks. The reason is that they buy high and often did so because they bought near the peak price - after the event that caused the price to react had occurred.

We tend to follow others, especially if they seem to be an authority, such as an investment analyst, stock commentator, or your favorite stock market 'guru' on social media. There is nothing wrong in listening to what others say, but you need to do your own due diligence by carrying out some research, and making your own decisions. I know it is easier said than done, hence, I'll provide ways to minimize the influence of emotions in your investing.

During bull markets, almost everyone is upbeat about the market. They buy and keep buying. Unfortunately, they continue to buy even when an asset appears to be overpriced. Their buying decisions are the result of advice from sources like television, newspapers, podcasts, social media, and friends. The excitement triggers the fear of missing out and most respond by buying. In their mind, they believe they are making rational decisions. After all, almost everyone is buying, they reason. Soon, the asset's price starts to decline and sets in motion the fear of losing. The bottom line is that emotional investing depends on fear and greed.

Why do investors, especially beginners, behave this way? There are two major reasons, namely, lack of the sufficient knowledge and forgetting about the big picture. Let's have a look at each for a better understanding.

Lack of the Right Knowledge

I am all for action. However, I prefer targeted action and informed decision making rather than acting blindly. I see beginner investors jumping into the game without doing the necessary preparations. They often don't take time to learn how the different markets work. It happens in all markets whether the stock market, commodities, cryptocurrencies, or foreign exchange. Sometimes, I don't blame them.

There are experienced investors who make investing look so easy that a 10-year-old without basic math skills could do it. Perhaps one in a million of such children could do it, but reality suggests otherwise. As it is often said in the personal development space, "Every master was once a beginner." This applies equally well in investing. The experienced investor made beginner mistakes and to their credit, they learned from them and discovered ways to win more often than they lose. At the back of all investing success lies the right knowledge.

You are already deep in the process of acquiring the right knowledge. Every beginner investor should know how the market works. In turn, they'll understand what makes asset prices move up and down, and differentiate noise from real market movements. This knowledge, coupled with fundamental and technical analyses, can enable investors to become and stay calm under varied market situations. Here are some of the errors that investors make due to a lack of accurate and sufficient knowledge.

- Investors know the importance of diversifying. Yet, there are many people who overweigh their portfolios with the stock of the company they work for. They probably do this because the companies provide retirement funds and stock incentives. This should not lead to avoidance of investing principles.

- Beginner investments usually don't understand how bonds work. As a result, they avoid adding them to their portfolios. Little do they know that bonds must be paid out first when the issuing company goes bankrupt. Furthermore, beginners are not aware that bond prices often drop when interest rates increase. You can take advantage of this when it occurs.

- Most investors do not know how to rebalance their portfolio when one of their assets increases or decreases substantially. So, they keep holding onto the asset instead of either selling or buying it. Selling would make money available to buy more promising assets that may have lagged.

So, having the right knowledge is key to investing success however, this doesn't work well alone as you need to deal with the next factor responsible for emotional investing.

Forgetting the Big Picture Perspective

It is common for most investors to claim that they invest for the long term. Yet, their actions and decisions reflect someone thinking about the short-term. For example, when an asset declines in price they begin to worry and fret. A long-term focused investor sets goals that show their perspective. The problem is that most investors do not create financial plans to achieve the long-term perspective they have in mind. This is a major issue because the up and down swings of the market can dictate their investment decisions.

It is not surprising that beginners and average investors usually buy more assets when the price is high. And, when the market declines, they panic and sell just when professionals begin to accumulate at low prices. So, staying on your long-term focus is the way to go. Importantly, set financial goals that reflect that perspective followed by congruent behaviors.

Now, having identified that emotions are the major barriers to investing success, how do you handle them? The next section provides the answers.

Ways to Remove Emotions Out of Your Investing Decisions

There are numerous ways of taking control over your investment decisions. One of the obvious is to gather the sufficient knowledge by thorough research before you select your assets, and stay on the chosen investment course even when things seem to change negatively in the short-term. If you made the right investment decision based on sound fundamental and technical analyses, you are likely to be right. In Chapter 3, I shared several keys to successful portfolio management. Keep them in mind when do your research.

Two more tools to attain control are through diversification and rebalancing; these are concepts that we also covered.

Let us take a look at other ways to control emotional investing.

Dollar-Cost Averaging (DCA)

Dollar-cost averaging involves dividing your investing money into portions for periodic buying of a given asset to reduce the risk and overall cost of the purchase. It is also called the *constant dollar plan*. The investor buys the asset at predetermined time intervals such as weekly, monthly, or quarterly. Surely, the price of the asset changes from day-to-day and there is a chance that you may buy when it is lower or higher than the first purchase.

The advantage of DCA is that you don't have to worry about the tiresome work of timing entry into the market. A good example of a DCA is the 401(k) plan in the United States. The employee regularly contributes a portion of their salary into the plan. That money is used to buy mutual funds or index funds to grow the capital for retirement purposes. However, you can employ the same strategy outside a 401(k) plan.

Let me illustrate with an example how this technique works. Suppose that you have $50,000 to invest in a certain stock currently selling for $85 a share. If you buy using the regular approach, you would make a once-off purchase of 588 shares, assuming you cannot purchase fractional shares. However, when you adopt the DCA, you could divide your capital by five to get

$10,000. Then, decide to buy the same stock weekly or whatever time interval you choose. We'll use weekly in this example. So, you'll buy the stock at roughly the same day and time every week.

Let's assume your purchases are as follows:

Week Number	Price per share	Number of Shares Bought
Week 1	85	117
Week 2	81	123
Week 3	86	116
Week 3	78	128
Week 5	82	122

In total, you would have bought 606 shares at approximately $50,000. This works out to an average share price of $82.51, which is cheaper than when buying all at a go. That's why you would have bought approximately 18 shares more. Do you see how advantageous DCA is? You should consider using it if you want to minimize the price you pay for a stock or any asset.

Track Your Performance

Investing is a process that consists of steps you would repeat each time you buy or sell. The effectiveness of each step can be evaluated by how the decision you make delivers on what you want. For example, you follow certain criteria when choosing the sector and stock to invest in. You should document all the steps that you take in making those decisions.

Over time, you'll have something like a checklist or a procedure to ensure that you select the right stock or asset to meet your objectives. The document may not be perfect at the beginning but as you refine it, it will become more effective. You can have a similar document for selecting commodities, foreign exchange, cryptocurrencies, and any other asset. What you then need is the discipline to follow your procedure when you buy or sell an asset. This way, you can take emotions out of your investing decisions. I like to call this a *policy of actions*.

Learn to Handle the Losses

There is no doubt that you will lose capital. Don't let this deter you because almost everyone loses capital at some point, especially at the beginning of their investing journey. In fact, failing to incorporate the possibility of a loss or more is a sign of misunderstanding how markets work. Give yourself room for making mistakes and learning from them.

You can minimize your losses by placing stop orders. This strategy is not an indication that you expect the price to drop. It is a sign that you know what could happen and taking the necessary precautions to protect your investment. However, you need to develop a sound strategy for placing the stop orders so that you don't trigger unnecessary selling. If you have a brokerage account that is self-directed, investigate how to set this up, if required, as most brokerages offer this feature.

The above are some of the ways to ensure you depend more on reason than emotion in investing. Following them will help you to stay calm and improve your chances of reaching your desired investing objectives.

Now, let's go over a summary of what we have discovered in this book.

CONCLUSION

You have now come up to speed with the process of successful investing. Some investors choose to hand over their hard-earned money to someone to invest for them. The problem is that people may not always be available to you. Besides, they won't be as involved in helping you as they would investing for themselves. This book contains the information that you needed to start investing for yourself and by yourself.

In a nutshell, successful investing involves the following steps:
- You choose and study the markets that you want to invest in.
- Next, you decide on your investment goals based on your risk tolerance. Only then can you start to research potential assets to include in your portfolio.
- Once you have built a portfolio, you need to manage it to ensure that it stays on course to deliver the results you want.
- Finally, you control your emotions to avoid making costly mistakes. In fact, emotions play a role throughout the investing process.

And a brief summary of each chapter that relates to each step of the investing process.

In Chapter 1, you learned about the different assets that you can potentially invest in - stocks, cryptocurrencies, exchange-traded funds, mutual funds, and bonds. When you own a stock of a company, you own part of the business. The percentage ownership will depend on the number of shares you own. You make money in stocks through dividends and capital gains. So, you should aim to buy at a price below the intrinsic or true value of a business to improve your chances of making money.

Cryptocurrencies are digital currencies that are free from control by entities such as the government. They are deflationary in nature so that their value depends on supply and demand. However, they are extremely volatile, making them better candidates for long-term investment. Bonds are debt securities issued by corporates and governments. They are relatively safe but offer low returns. Exchange-traded funds and mutual funds allow for effortless diversification. Most of them don't beat the stock market, but a good choice can be a savvy investment decision.

One of the key decisions we discussed is to select an appropriate brokerage account. Your investment needs, personal situation, and objectives should guide in the account selection process. In your search for the account, ensure that you evaluate and compare factors such as expenses, account features, services, and incentives. Once you have decided on the right firm, go ahead and apply for an account. Only then, can you fund the account through available means that may include electronic fund transfers (EFTs) and wire transfers, which can be automated or manual. Armed with these basics, you move on to the next step of the process.

That's where Chapter 2 came in to show you how to go about selecting assets for your investment portfolio. The first thing you discovered was the importance of setting your specific, measurable, achievable, realistic, and time-based investment goals. You need to do this because it helps work out your risk tolerance, something necessary for selecting relevant securities. When you know your risk tolerance, build a portfolio that considers your risk tolerance to deliver on your goals.

The next task we talked about was selecting the assets to include in your investment portfolio. You need to value the asset, especially stocks, so that you can determine if the asset is at a discount or not. Buying at a discount is a sure way to make money right when you buy. This is where fundamental analysis comes in. In deciding when to buy, you employ technical analysis. A good brokerage account may provide analyst recommendations, stock valuations, and other expert financial advice that may be helpful.

When selecting assets, ensure that you diversify by industry, asset, and financial market; this process is called diversification. The main idea is to minimize risk exposure and maximize returns. The chapter concluded by giving ideas on how to select stocks, bonds, cryptocurrencies, and ETFs. When you have completed the building of your portfolio, you move on to managing it.

Managing your portfolio was covered in Chapter 3. There, you discovered the major reasons for portfolio management. This process begins when you set investment goals and determine your risk tolerance. It culminates into two major processes - monitoring and rebalancing. The reasons you monitor your portfolio is to catch it when it shifts away from your asset allocation and diversification position. Such a change, if not caught early and adjusted, could result in a vastly different portfolio from the one that you originally planned for.

Changes, such as market cycles and personal circumstances, could necessitate the rebalancing of your portfolio. Rebalancing is the process of selling the highest-performing asset and buying more of the low-performing securities. This helps dilute the highest-performing asset so that you maintain the risk level that you can deal with. One option of rebalancing involves adding more money into your portfolio and buying more of the lowest-performing assets. This produces the same effect and could reduce transaction costs. However, ensure that you check which of the two processes is cheaper to perform. Don't forget that expenses can be costly to you over the long term. Some of the costs to consider include taxes. When you sell assets, you may attract capital gains tax depending on the account where your assets are domiciled. If you get interest income, it may be taxed at your marginal tax rate. So, ensure you plan your taxes so that you make decisions that minimize the amounts that you pay.

The book wouldn't have been complete without dealing with the psychology of investing. Chapter 4 dealt with this important subject in detail. The most important aspect of investing is handling your emotions, especially fear and greed. You need to ensure that you have the right knowledge and information when you make investing decisions. There are many investors who follow what they see and hear others doing. Even if you get investing recommendations, do your due diligence to ensure that the asset meets *your* investment criteria.

Keep reminding yourself of the big picture and the major reason why you decided to invest. This will help you to stay grounded and maintain the investment course you have chosen. Using strategies like the dollar-cost averaging can save you money and minimize the impact of market volatility. Most importantly, learn to handle losses because it is part of investing. All this information will give you a good head start in Investing as a beginner. If you follow the ideas, concepts, and tips shared in this book, you will invest with confidence and achieve most of your investment goals. Experienced investors often repeat their investing approaches over and over.

Happy Investing!

REFERENCES

Best, R. (2020, May 24). Put $10,000 in the S&P 500 ETF and wait 20 years. Investopedia. https://www.investopedia.com/articles/personal-finance/022216/put-10000-sp-500-etf-and-wait-20-years.asp

CoinMarketCap. (n.d.). Global cryptocurrency charts. CoinMarketCap. https://coinmarketcap.com/charts/

Crunch. (2021, March 5). UK tax rates, thresholds & allowances for 2018/2019 and 2019/20. Crunch. https://www.crunch.co.uk/knowledge/tax/tax-rates-thresholds-and-allowances-for-current-tax-year/

Dogen, S. (2019, April 25). Historical returns of different stock and bond portfolio weightings. Financial Samurai. https://www.financialsamurai.com/historical-returns-of-different-stock-bond-portfolio-weightings/

Godfrey, H. (2021, February 19). Bitcoin boom delivers cryptocurrency $1 trillion market cap. CityA.M. https://www.cityam.com/bitcoin-boom-delivers-cryptocurrency-1-trillion-market-cap/

O'Hara, N. (2020, September 25). Investment tax basics for all investors. Investopedia. https://www.investopedia.com/articles/investing/072313/investment-tax-basics-all-investors.asp RBC Global Asset Management. (n.d.). Understanding taxes and your investments.

RBC Global Asset Management. https://www.rbcgam.com/en/ca/learn-plan/investment-basics/understanding-taxes-and-your-investments/detail

BitDegree. (2021, January 6). Best cryptocurrency to Invest 2021—The complete guide. BitDegree. https://www.bitdegree.org/crypto/best-cryptocurrency

SoFi Learn. (2021, January 6). How often you should rebalance your investments. SoFi. https://www.sofi.com/learn/content/when-to-rebalance-portfolio/ the Money Advice Service. (n.d.). Tax on savings and investments—how it works.

The Money Advice Service. https://www.moneyadviceservice.org.uk/en/articles/your-tax-rate

Thune, K. (2020, December 30). What is the average mutual fund return? The Balance. https://www.thebalance.com/what-is-the-average-mutual-fund-return-4773782